4

CHORAL MUSIC

SATB double choir and organ

OXFORD

Coronation Te Deum

William Walton

Version for choir and organ

by

Simon Preston and Mark Blatchly

MUSIC DEPARTMENT

OXFORD
UNIVERSITY PRESS

Coronation Te Deum

Arranged by Simon Preston
Organ reduction by Mark Blatchly

WILLIAM WALTON

* *f* and *ff* refer to an essential distinction, not so much in volume but to that of 8′ + 4′ on the one hand and 8′ + 4′ + 2′ + mixtures on the other.

Composed for the Coronation of Her Majesty Queen Elizabeth II in Westminster Abbey, 2 June 1953. The vocal parts have been slightly rearranged to facilitate performance by smaller choirs. The original version, with accompaniment for full orchestra and organ and a slightly fuller disposition of the voice parts, is also available (orchestral material on hire). An accompaniment for 4 trumpets, 4 trombones, and organ is available on hire.

© Oxford University Press 1988

Printed in Great Britain

OXFORD UNIVERSITY PRESS, MUSIC DEPARTMENT, GREAT CLARENDON STREET, OXFORD OX2 6DP

6

the Heavens, and all the Powers there-in.

the Heavens, and all the Powers there-in.

the Heavens, and all the Powers there-in.

the Heavens, and all the Powers there-in.

(Ped.)

CHOIR 1 **3** **più animato** (♩. = 58-60)

mp *cresc.*

To thee Che-ru-bin, and

mp *cresc.*

To thee Che-ru-bin, and

mp *cresc.*

To thee Che-ru-bin, and

mp *cresc.*

To thee Che-ru-bin, and

3 **più animato** (♩. = 58-60) Gt.

Sw. *fp* *cresc.*

7

8

* Whenever possible, this part should be sung by a counter-tenor.

full of the Ma - jes - ty of___ thy___ glo - ry,

full of the Ma - jes - ty of thy glo - ry,

full of the Ma - jes - ty of___ thy___ glo - ry,

full of the Ma - jes - ty of thy glo - ry,

Heaven and earth are

Heaven and earth are

Heaven and earth are

Heaven and earth are

12

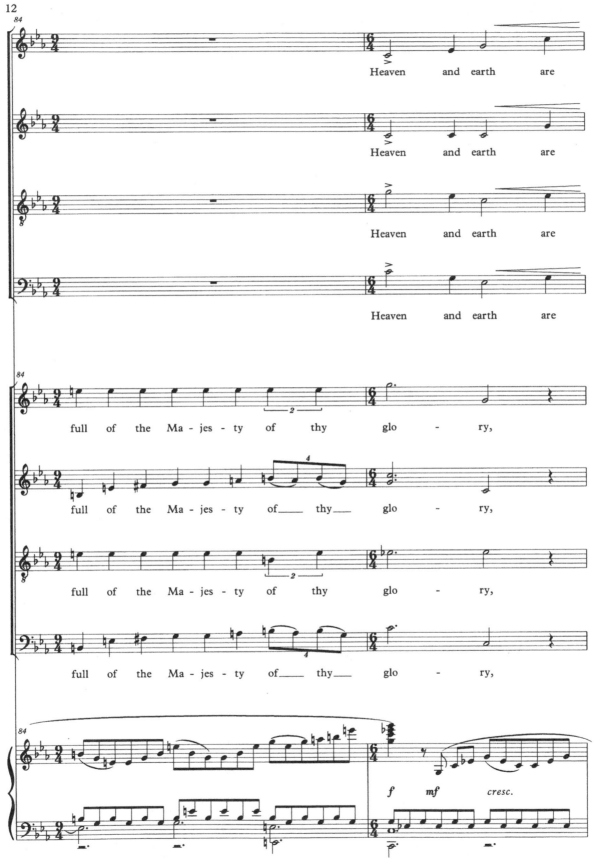

Heaven and earth are full of the Ma - jes - ty of thy glo - ry,

* Whenever possible, these parts should be sung by boys only.

16

18

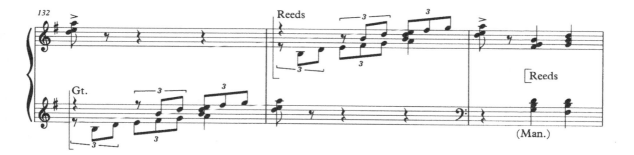

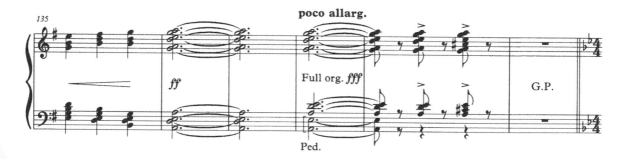

9 Risoluto (poco meno mosso: ♩= c.116)
S.
A.
T.
B.
Thou art the King of Glory, O Christ. Thou
Thou art the King of Glory, O Christ. Thou
Thou art the King of Glory, O Christ. Thou
Thou art the King of Glory, O Christ. Thou
9 Risoluto (poco meno mosso: ♩= c.116)
Gt. ff
Reeds
Ped.
-32′
sub. a tempo vivo (♩= c.126)
art the ev - er - last - ing Son of the Fa -
art the ev - er - last - ing Son of the Fa -
art the ev - er - last - ing Son of the Fa -
art the ev - er - last - ing Son of the Fa -
sub. a tempo vivo (♩= c.126)
(Gt.)
Sw. ff
Gt.
f
f

ther.

ther.

ther.

ther.

dim.

pp

24

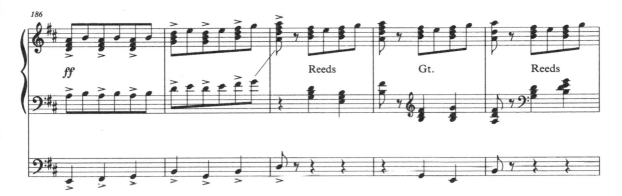

28

30

pochiss. allarg.

Day by day we mag - ni - fy thee;

Day by day we mag - ni - fy thee;

Day by day we mag - ni - fy thee;

Day by day we mag - ni - fy thee;

pochiss. allarg.

ff marcatissimo

wor - ship thy name, And we

ff marcatissimo

wor - ship thy name, And we

ff marcatissimo

wor - ship thy name, And we

ff marcatissimo

wor - ship thy name, And we

pochiss. allarg.

f *mf* *cresc.* (Gt.)

*Whenever possible, these parts should be sung by boys only.

36

Music origination by Barnes Music Engraving, East Sussex
Printed by Halstan & Co. Ltd., Amersham, Bucks., England

WALTON

Coronation Te Deum

ISBN 978-0-19-353487-